I0617448

THE TEN COMMANDMENTS in *POETRY*

THE ROCKEFELLER COLLECTION

WRITTEN By BILL ROCKEFELLER

PURPOSELY DRIVEN POEMS
Volume II

Battle Press
SATELLITE BEACH, FLORIDA

THE TEN COMMANDMENTS in *POETRY*

The Rockefeller Collection, Volume II

Books may be ordered through booksellers or by visiting:

bill@purposelydrivenpoems.com
Purposelydrivenpoems.com

Or contact:

Battle Press
steve@battlepress.media
www.battlepress.media

ISBN: 979-8-9873-3790-5 (SC)
ISBN: 979-8-9873-3791-2 (HC)
ISBN: 979-8-9873-3792-9 (eBook)

LCCN: 2023905894

First Edition

THE TEN COMMANDMENTS

The foundation of your moral
and spiritual compass
to guide your truth and your way.

They came straight from our God
do we remember what they say?

They are rules to control your decisions
that better our humanity.

These words direct from Almighty God
a small list for you and me.

PSALM 11:3
When the foundations are being destroyed
what can the righteous do?

PURPOSELYDRIVENPOEMS.COM

CONTENTS

INTRODUCTION

We all need daily directions
To move us throughout the day
If we use a moral compass
our righteousness won't slip away
The guidelines from our father
were meant to help us grow
Together as brothers and sisters
with the moral compass you hold
We know it's never so easy
But we realize it's never that hard
When you're guided by your moral compass
and your heart is led by God

Ambassador to Jesus

BILL ROCKEFELLER

PUPOSELYDRIVENPOEMS.COM

1st COMMANDMENT
THOU SHALL HAVE NO OTHER GODS
BEFORE ME

OUR GOD

One God one life
Each day
to live it right
he who watches from above
the father of all stars
sends out his grace and mercy
which spreads his words so far
no one could ever
equal his virtue
no matter how good you are
but everyone knows his name
that's why he is
Our God

PURPOSELYDRIVENPOEMS.COM

2nd COMMANDMENT
THOU SHALL NOT MAKE UNTO THEE ANY GRAVEN IMAGE

We worship our God in spirit
we worship God with prayer
we worship God with praise
his motives fill our air
we worship God in action
we worship God with care
we follow his Commandments
for his love is everywhere
he doesn't need a logo
or a fancy NFT
just his power to reach our spirit
so no false idol
could ever be

PURPOSELYDRIVENPOEMS.COM

3rd COMMANDMENT
YOU SHALL NOT TAKE THE NAME OF YOUR
GOD IN VAIN

VAIN

The name of God is precious
and anointed just the same
with all he's given us today
you need not
use his name in vain
your blame is not on Him
His blame is not on you
His words and steps
of guidance
are yours
to always
pull you through

PURPOSELYDRIVENPOEMS.COM

4th COMMANDMENT
REMEMBER THE SABBATH DAY TO KEEP IT HOLY

The path of life is busy
it tricks you for the treats
as a rose by any other name
would always smell as sweet
each day we breathe a heartbeat
it keeps us so alive
if ever it was to stop
could our life be
summarized
holy are the days we breathe
we laugh we cry
keep the sabbath holy to
thank God we are still alive

PURPOSELYDRIVENPOEMS.COM

5th COMMANDMENT
HONOR THY FATHER AND THY MOTHER
THAT THEIR DAYS BE LONG

HONOR

We all come from our mother
she brought us here today
God created our life to continue
with love and a spiritual way
our parents carried us for years
while blessing
kept falling from our Lord
we must honor our only parents
who raised us from the floor
when we give it thought
it's really not too hard
they were our 1st genetic gift
right from our
Father God

PURPOSELYDRIVENPOEMS.COM

6th Commandment
Thou Shall Not Kill

Kill

Life is for the living
death is for the done
arrows or bullets
designed for our protection
should never kill anyone
we live this life so fruitful
each day we rise with the sun
we have not the right
to ever kill this joy
from anyone living under the light
of the Lord God's sun

PURPOSELYDRIVENPOEMS.COM

7th COMMANDMENT
THOU SHALL NOT COMMIT ADULTERY

If you're committed to one person
like a marriage vow would claim
then keep this reputation
not to bring it down to shame
it affects more than two people
adultery can stain
the sacred white
condition of marriage
to bring all involved some pain
so leave those temptations
stagnant and far away
to be blessed
by the marriage prayer
that you both chose
to share today

PURPOSELYDRIVENPOEMS.COM

8th COMMANDMENT
THOU SHALL NOT STEAL

What's yours is yours

now I say unless a thief

comes and steals it away

if it was yours

and yours was real

How then would your loss

really feel

I say again

if it happened to you

would you pass it forward

to someone new

ponder the thought

back in your mind

to steal is wrong

and never kind

PURPOSELYDRIVENPOEMS.COM

9th COMMANDMENT
THOU SHALL NOT BEAR WITNESS
AGAINST THY NEIGHBOUR

NEIGHBOUR

The truth is a reminder
Of how
you should act
a witness is great
to compliment the facts
people gather together
depend on each other
to grow and harmonize
as sisters and brothers
before you choose
to adjust this true life fact
if you're a false witness
against your neighbour
your friendships won't last

PURPOSELYDRIVENPOEMS.COM

10th COMMANDMENT
THOU SHALL NOT COVET

Jealousy comes
but can be controlled
some people have more
then others we know
we all stand here
to prosper and grow
with many thoughts
and more actions to go
incisively designed to generate our flow
with the low inspiration
impersonal drops of sweat
my neighbours house
I will never ever have to covet

PURPOSELYDRIVENPOEMS.COM

A LITTLE HUG

I was born on this planet without a care
God knew as I grew
I would have a lot to share
to all who read these poems of life
I hope they bring you a smile and delight
I wrote these poems for the fortunate few
who read with feeling just like you
yet since my time will soon be gone
I hope you enjoy them, and they carry on
not knowing when our spirits might meet
if you can't send me an email or a tweet
if you arrive in heaven up above
Just give my spirit
a little hug

PSALMS 18:23
Though he had commanded the clouds
from up above,
and opened the doors to heaven.

PURPOSELYDRIVENPOEMS.COM

EVERY DAY

We live our lives as angels
flying so carefully
touching
all the hearts
that ever come to be
our each and every moment
is opulent in time
to keep us moving forward
with every day we find

Matthew 6:11
Give us this day our daily bread.

PURPOSELYDRIVENPOEMS.COM

HOPE

Hope is a word

so small and so fine

Hope is the word

to inspire your mind

Hope is the feeling

that helps you to grow

very easy to take around

anywhere you go

ROMANS 15:13
*Now the God of hope shall fill you with all
the joy and peace in believing that ye
may abound in hope.*

PURPOSELYDRIVENPOEMS.COM

OUR PURPOSE

God created a plan
for each one of us
in our beautiful life
called the human purpose
he knew from the beginning
we would find the right purpose
at the right time
it would hold truth
in our hearts and mind
other's too would find
their own in time
it's all for one and one for all
when your human purpose
gives you a call
in our own way
we each feel our truth
it speaks to us each day
it started in our youth.

EPHESIANS 1:11
*In whom also we have obtained an inheritance
predestined according to the purpose of him
who worketh all things after the counsel
of his own will.*

PURPOSELYDRIVENPOEMS.COM

SMART I PHONE

God's got your number
you are never alone,
He could reach you through
your smart Iphone.
He knows your every call,
He has your back in case you fall
He loves your honor in circumstances
to always give you another chance
Wear His armor, wear it proud
so you won't be taken down
Keep your faith, be it known,
God's got your back, you're never alone
He could reach you through
your Smart IPhone

ISAIAH 30:21
*Whether you turn to the right or to the left
your ears will hear a voice behind you saying
this is the way, walk in it.*

PURPOSELYDRIVENPOEMS.COM

PEACE

There is peace in Jesus
enough to cover the world
for every living boy
and every special girl
he is a ďivine spirit
to shòw promise
from his father to be
to show this world
how to live in harmony
feel the peace
it can be in your life
every day every night

JOHN 14:27
Peace I leave with you
my peace I give unto you
not as the world gives
us give I unto you let not
your heart be troubled
neither let it be afraid

PURPOSELYDRIVENPOEMS.COM

TEMPTATIONS

Temptation comes
when it does
we must act
like it never was
we must stand strong so
it never can be
the temptations
to distract
from our destiny

Ephesians 6:11

Put on the whole armor of God
that you may be able
to stand against the wile
temptations of the devil

Inspired by
Pastor Joel Olsteen

PURPOSELYDRIVENPOEMS.COM

SPIRIT OF LIFE

The spirit of life
lives in us all
the more we believe
the less we will fall
and the greater we will feel
about it all
God helps us with directions
that are easy to follow
so we can grow up
not to be spiritually shallow
our Faith provides
dynamic confidence
so everywhere we go
our spirit of life
is the star of the show

JOHN 6:63
It is the spirit who gives life,
the flesh provides nothing.
The words I speak unto you
they are spirit and they are life.

THE LORD'S DAY

The path of life is busy
It tricks you with the treats
as a rose by any other name
would always smell as sweet

Each day we breathe our heartbeats
it keeps us so alive
if ever it was to stop
could our life be summarized?

Holy are all the days we dance
we laugh we cry
keep the sabbath Holy
to thank God you're still alive

Remember to keep Holy the Lord's day

PURPOSELYDRIVENPOEMS.COM

Order the Wall Poem of your choice in Canvas to hang on your wall and inspire your home. Check out the entire selection of Wall Poems at:

PURPOSELYDRIVENPOEMS.COM

FAITH Wall Poem

***AMEN* Wall Poem**

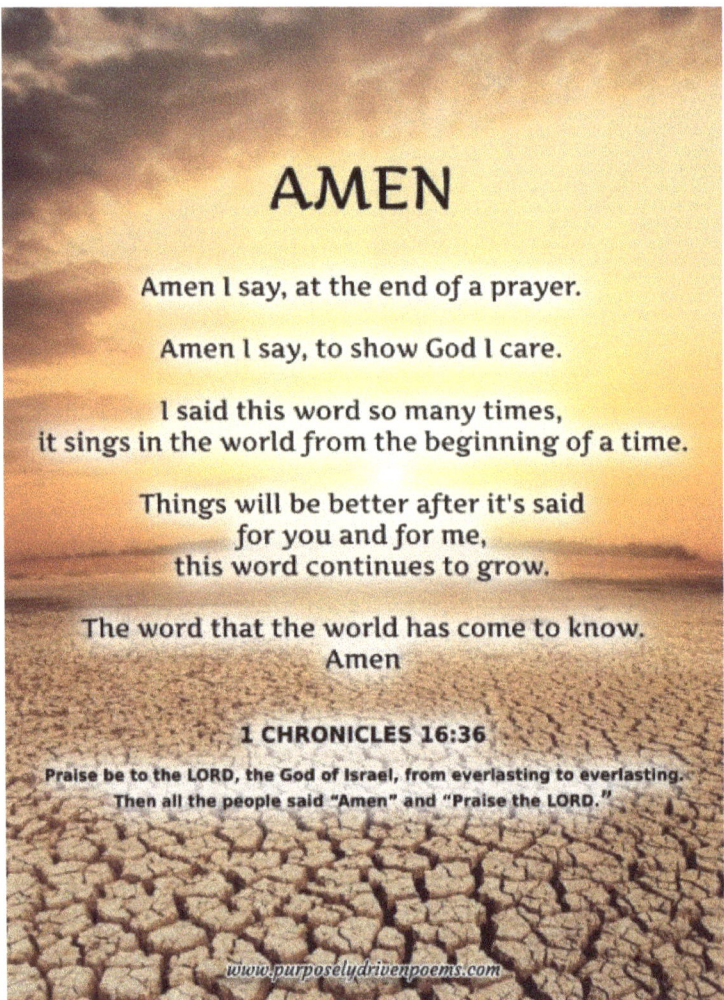

PURPOSELYDRIVENPOEMS.COM

Puposely Driven Poems Volume 1 **is Bill Rockefeller's first book.** The book showcases 100 additional poems to inspire you. Available on Amazon, Barnes & Noble, and Battle Press: https://battlepress.media/?product=purposely-driven-poems

PURPOSELYDRIVENPOEMS.COM

If you enjoyed this book, please take a few moments to write a review, and refer it to anyone you know who may enjoy it.

I welcome questions or comments.

Please Email:

Bill Rockefeller

bill@purposelydrivenpoems.com

and

visit my Website:

PURPOSELYDRIVENPOEMS.COM

www.ingramcontent.com/pod-product-compliance
Lightning Source LLC
Chambersburg PA
CBHW040513150626
46551CB00033B/2635